American Folk Songs

for Voice and Piano
1 or 2 vocal parts

20 Traditional Pieces

Edited and arranged by Philip Lawson

With accompanying CD

ED 13843
ISMN 979-0-2201-3687-0
ISBN 978-1-84761-473-5

www.schott-music.com

Mainz · London · Madrid · Berlin · New York · Paris · Prague · Tokyo · Toronto
© 2016 SCHOTT MUSIC Ltd, London · Printed in Germany

CD recording credits

Soprano: Sophie Lawson
Baritone: Philip Lawson
Piano: Andrew Post and Philip Lawson

Recorded and edited by Andrew Post

ED 13843
British Library Cataloguing-in-Publication Data.
A catalogue record for this book is available from the British Library

ISMN 979-0-2201-3687-0
ISBN 978-1-84761-473-5

© 2016 Schott Music Ltd, London

French translation: Michaëla Rubi
German translation: Heike Brühl
Design and typesetting by www.adamhaystudio.com
Cover photography: iStockphoto.com
Music setting and page layout by Scott Barnard (www.musicpreparation.co.uk)
Printed in Germany S&Co. 9277

Contents

The Pieces

Introduction

Here is the fourth in my series of upper voice folksongs. Some of the material inevitably derives from British folksongs that were imported with the settlers, but a significant proportion is indigenous and contains spiritual songs arising out of the oppressed slave population, and often highly partisan battle songs from the years of the Civil War.

My first few arrangements of folk songs were done in the 1980s for a vocal quartet I was in at the time, but the majority of my work in this field has been a number of fairly complicated six-part arrangements for The King's Singers, with whom I performed for 18 years. My aim for the two-part versions in this collection has been to maintain simplicity in the vocal lines, but develop some interest in the accompaniments. Most of the songs may be sung in unison if necessary.

It is my hope that the collection might help to introduce future generations to some of the wonderful literature, both verbal and musical, which forms our folk song heritage, and might inspire them to explore it further.

Please note that the songs are all intended to be performed by equal-pitched upper voices, despite the use of soprano and baritone on the recording.

About the Author

Philip Lawson sang baritone with The King's Singers from 1993 to 2012. While with the group he was their principal arranger, contributing more than 50 arrangements to the repertoire, including 10 for the 2008 CD *Simple Gifts* which went on to win a GRAMMY for Best Classical Crossover Album in 2009. Philip now has over 200 published works. In addition to his writing and arranging he leads workshops in Europe and the US. He works in the Vocal Departments of Wells Cathedral School, Salisbury Cathedral School and the University of Bristol, and has recently been appointed Director of Music of The Romsey Singers
www.philiplawson.net

Introduction

Voici le quatrième volume de ma collection consacrée à la chanson traditionnelle pour voix élevées. Importés par les premiers colons, certains matériaux musicaux puisent inévitablement leurs racines dans le répertoire traditionnel britannique, mais une proportion significative d'entre eux sont d'origine locale, qu'il s'agisse de spirituals nés de l'oppression des esclaves ou de chants de guerre souvent très partisans remontant à la guerre de Sécession.

Datant des années 1980, mes premiers arrangements de chansons populaires étaient destinés à un quatuor vocal dont j'étais membre à ce moment-là. Mais dans ce domaine, j'ai effectué la majeure partie de mon travail pour les King's Singers avec qui j'ai chanté pendant 18 ans et pour lesquels j'écrivais des arrangements à 6 voix relativement complexes. Mon objectif dans la version à deux voix proposée ici a été de préserver la simplicité des lignes vocales toutw en développant un certain intérêt pour l'accompagnement. La plupart des chansons peuvent être chantées à l'unisson si nécessaire.

J'espère que ce recueil permettra de faire connaître aux générations futures un répertoire merveilleux, dont les paroles et la musique constituent notre héritage de chansons populaires, et qu'il les incitera continuer à l'explorer.

À propos de l'auteur

Baryton au sein des King's Singers de 1993 à 2012, Philip Lawson fut aussi leur arrangeur principal pendant cette période, apportant plus de 50 arrangements à leur répertoire, y compris 10 des titres du CD *Simple Gifts* paru en 2008 qui obtint le GRAMMY du Best Classical Crossover Album en 2009. Aujourd'hui, Philip peut se targuer de plus de 200 œuvres éditées. Outre ses activités de compositeur et d'arrangeur, il encadre de nombreux stages en Europe et aux USA et travaille au département voix de la Wells Cathedral School, de la Salisbury Cathedral School et de l'université de Bristol. Il a été nommé récemment directeur musical des Romsey Singers.
www.philiplawson.net

Einleitung

Hier ist der vierte Band meiner Folksong-Reihe für hohe Stimmen. Einige Stücke stammen natürlich von britischen Folksongs ab, die von den Siedlern mitgebracht wurden. Die meisten Stücke sind jedoch „echt" amerikanisch, darunter Spirituals der unterdrückten Sklaven sowie leidenschaftliche Songs aus der Widerstandsbewegung zur Zeit des Bürgerkriegs.

Meine ersten Folksong-Arrangements entstanden in den 1980er-Jahren für ein Gesangsquartett, dem ich damals angehörte. Der Großteil meiner Arbeit als Arrangeur bestand jedoch in ziemlich komplizierten sechsstimmigen Bearbeitungen für die King's Singers, mit denen ich 18 Jahre lang auftrat. Mein Ziel für die zweistimmigen Versionen in dieser Sammlung war es, einfache Gesangsstimmen mit einer abwechslungsreichen Begleitung anzubieten. Die meisten Songs können auch einstimmig gesungen werden.

Ich hoffe, dass die Sammlung dazu beiträgt, zukünftigen Generationen möglichst viele Stücke aus unserem reichhaltigen Folksong-Repertoire zugänglich zu machen und sie anzuregen, sich auch weiterhin damit zu beschäftigen.

Der Autor

Philip Lawson war von 1993 bis 2012 Bariton bei den King's Singers. In dieser Zeit arrangierte er die meisten Stücke der Gruppe und steuerte über 50 Arrangements zu ihrem Repertoire bei, darunter zehn für die CD *Simple Gifts* von 2008, die 2009 einen Grammy in der Kategorie „Bestes klassisches Crossover-Album" gewann. Lawson hat mittlerweile über 200 Werke veröffentlicht. Wenn er nicht gerade komponiert und arrangiert, leitete er Workshops in Europa und den USA. Er arbeitet am Vocal Department der Wells Cathedral School und an der Universität Bristol und wurde kürzlich zum Chefdirigenten der Romsey Singers ernannt.
www.philiplawson.net

1. All the Pretty Little Horses

Traditional
Arr. Philip Lawson

hush - a - bye, don't you cry: Go to sleep, my lit-tle ba - by.

hush - a - bye, don't you cry: Go to sleep, my lit-tle ba - by.

Go to sleep, my lit-tle ba - by.

Go to sleep, my lit-tle ba - by.

2. Buffalo Gals

John Hodges (1844)
Arr. Philip Lawson

Performance:
Verse 1, Voice 1
Verse 2, Voice 2
Verse 3, Voice 1
Verse 4, Voice 2

1. As

(1.) I was wal-king down the street, down the street, down the street, A pret - ty girl I
(2.) asked her if she'd have a dance, have a dance, have a dance, I thought that I would

(1.) chanced to meet, and we danced by the light of the moon.
(2.) have a chance to___ shake a foot with_ her.

Buf-fa-lo gals won't you come out to-night,

come out to-night, come out to-night, Buf-fa-lo gals won't you come out to-night, and

3. Bright Sunny South

Traditional
Arr. Philip Lawson

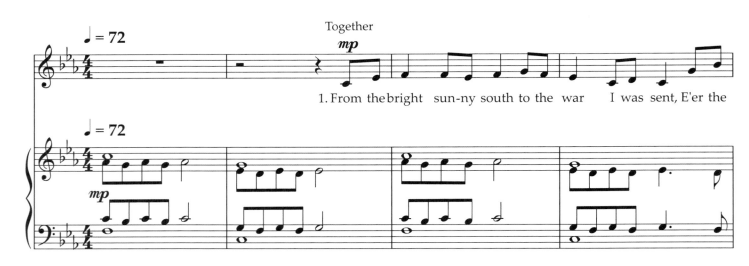

1. From the bright sun-ny south to the war I was sent, E'er the

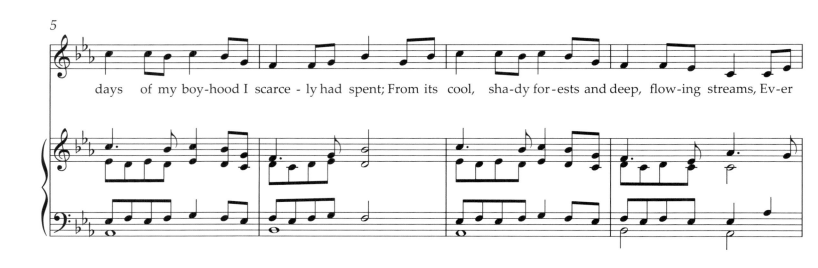

days of my boy-hood I scarce - ly had spent; From its cool, sha-dy for-ests and deep, flow-ing streams, Ev-er

fond in my mem-ory and sweet in my dreams.
2. Oh, my

dear lit-tle sis - ter, I still see her tears, When I had to leave home in
(3.) kind - heart-ed fa - ther as he took my hand: "As you go in de-fence of our

our ten - der years, And my sweet gen - tle mo - ther, so dear to my heart, It
dear na - tive land, Son, be brave but show mer - cy when - ev - er you can, Our

1. **2.**

grieved me sin-cere - ly when we had to part. 3. Said my
hearts will be with you 'til you turn a - gain.

4. In my bag there's a bi-ble to show me the way, Through my tri - als on earth, and to

Hea - ven some day, I will shoul - der my mus-ket and bran - dish my sword, In de-fence of this land, and the

word of the Lord.

rit.

4. Deep River

Traditional
Arr. Philip Lawson

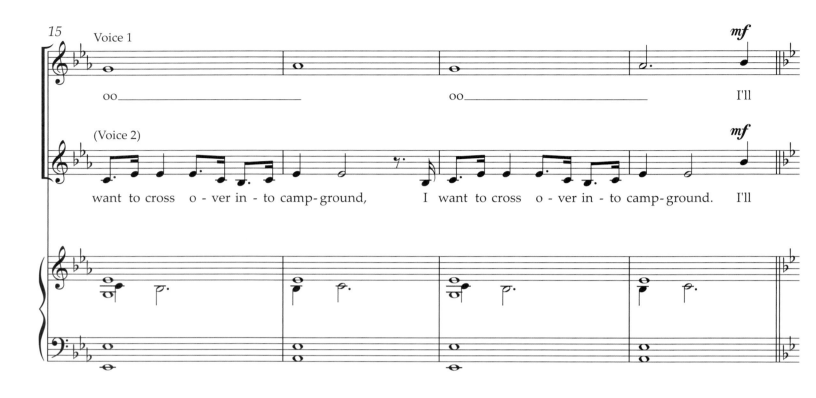

(5)

5. Dink's Song

Traditional
Arr. Philip Lawson

lis-tened to what my ma-ma___ said, I'd be at home in my ma-ma's___ bed. Fare thee

well, oh_____ hon-ey,___ fare___ thee well, fare___ thee

well.

6. Dixie

Daniel Emmett
Arr. Philip Lawson

1. I___ wish I was_ in the land of cot-ton,
2. There's buck-wheat cakes and_ In - jun bat - ter,

Old times there are not for-got-ten,
Makes you fat or a lit - tle fat-ter, } Look a - way, look a - way, look a -

- way,_____ Di - xie-land.
In___ Dix - ie - land_ where I was born in,
Then_ hoe it down and_ scratch your gra - vel, To

-way down south in Dix-ie, -way down south in Dix-ie, A - way, A - way, A -

-way down south in Dix-ie, -way down south in Dix-ie, A - way, A - way, A -

-way down south in Dix-ie, A - way, A - way, A - way down south in Dix - ie.

-way down south in Dix-ie, A - way, A - way, A - way down south in Dix - ie.

7. Jimmy Crack Corn

Traditional
Arr. Philip Lawson

Performance:
Verse 1, Voice 1
Verse 2, Voice 2
Verse 3, Voice 1
Verse 4, Voice 2
Verse 5, Voice 1

1. When I was young I
(2.) when he'd ride in the
(3.) day he rode a -
(4.) po - ny ran, he
(5.) laid him un - der a

used to wait up - on my boss, and give him his plate; And
_af - ter - noon, I'd fol - low be - hind with a hick - o - ry broom; The
round the farm, the flies so num' - rous they did swarm; One
jumped, he pitched, he threw my mas - ter in the ditch; He
'sim - mon tree, his ep - i - taph is there to see: "Be -

pass the bot - tle when he got dry, and brush a - way the blue - tail fly.
po - ny be - ing ra - ther shy, when bit - ten by the blue - tail fly.
chanced to bite him on the thigh, the dev - il take the blue - tail fly.
died; the ju - ry won - dered why, the ver - dict was the blue - tail fly.
-neath this stone I'm forced to lie, a vic - tim of the blue - tail fly".

8. I Bought Me a Cat

Traditional
Arr. Philip Lawson

* These last sounds may be omitted, or done randomly, if the rhythms prove difficult

9. Joshua Fought the Battle of Jericho

Traditional
Arr. Philip Lawson

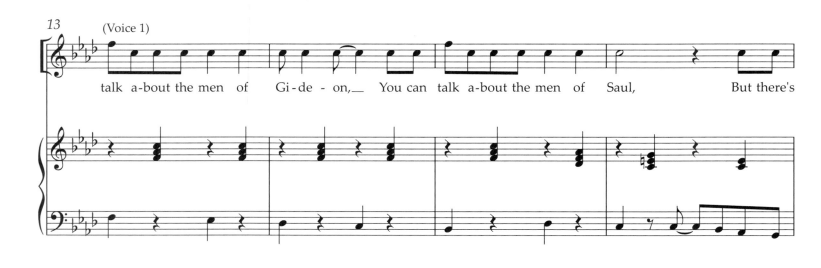

talk a-bout the men of Gi-de-on,__ You can talk a-bout the men of Saul, But there's

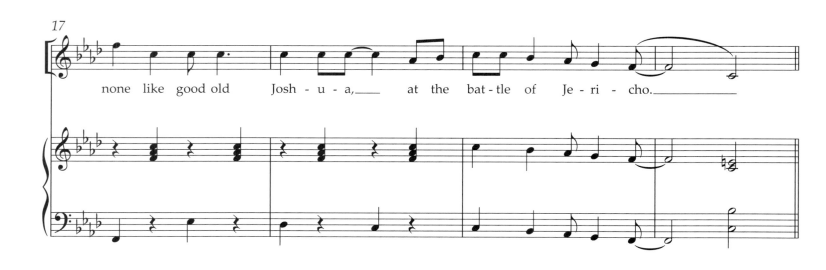

none like good old Josh-u-a,__ at the bat-tle of Je-ri-cho._____

(Voice 1)

Josh-ua fought the bat-tle of__ Je-ri-cho,__ Je-ri-cho,__ Je-ri-cho,__

Voice 2

Josh-ua fought the bat-tle of__ Je-ri-cho,__ Je-ri-cho,__ Je-ri-cho,__

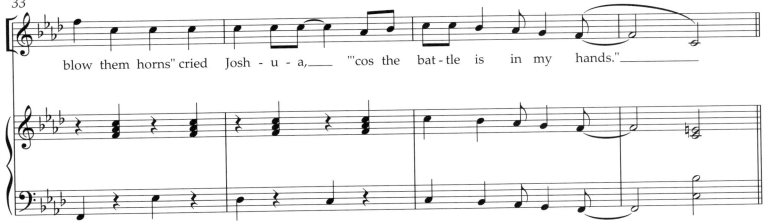

10. Marching Through Georgia

Henry Clay Work (1832-1884)
Arr. Philip Lawson

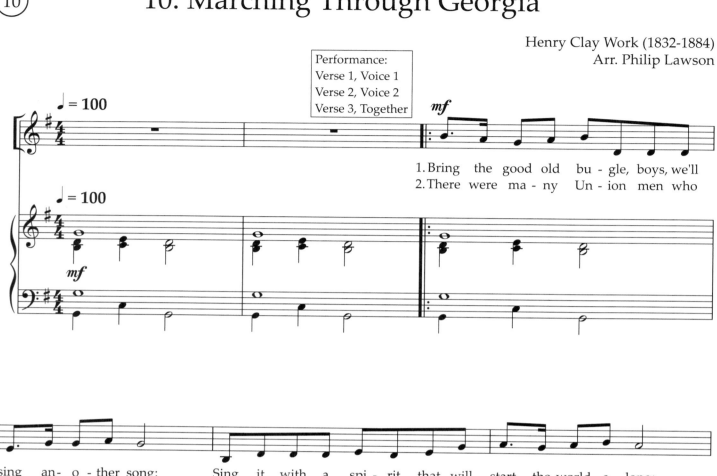

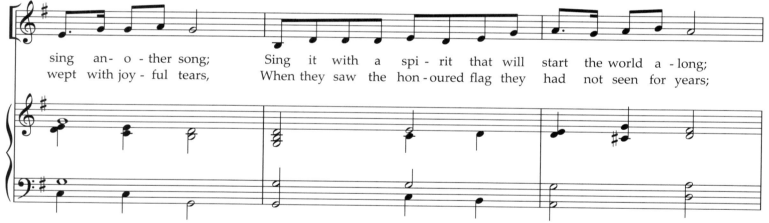

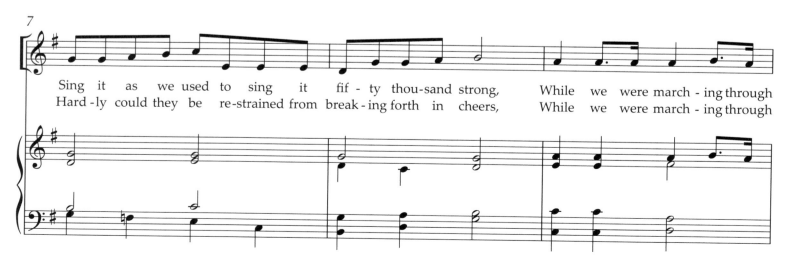

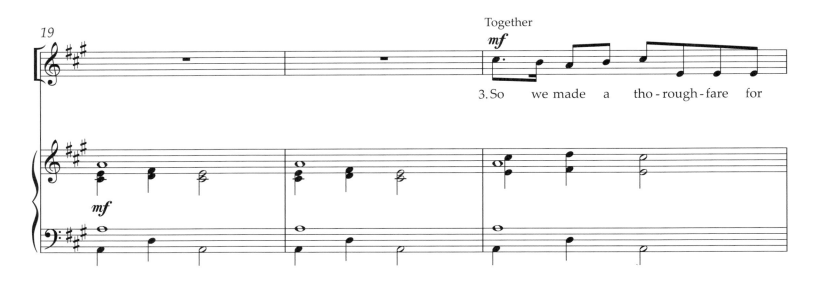

3. So we made a tho-rough-fare for

free-dom and her train, Six-ty miles in lat-i-ude, three hun-dred to the main;

Trea-son fled be-fore us, for re-sis-tance was in vain, While we were march-ing through

11. Michael, Row the Boat Ashore

Stephen Foster (1826-1864)
Arr. Philip Lawson

(3.) blow the trum-pet horn, Hal-le - lu - - jah; Ga-briel blow the trum-pet horn, Hal-le - lu -
(4.) sounds the ju - bi - lee, Hal-le - lu - - jah; Trum-pet sounds for you and me, Hal-le - lu -

(3.) blow the trum-pet horn, Hal-le - lu - - jah; Ga-briel blow the trum-pet horn, Hal-le - lu -
(4.) sounds the ju - bi - lee, Hal-le - lu - - jah; Trum-pet sounds for you and me, Hal-le - lu -

-jah. 4. Trum-pet 5. Jor-dan ri - ver's deep and wide, Hal - le - lu - jah;
-jah. -jah.

-jah. 4. Trum-pet -jah.
And my

row the boat a - shore, Hal - le - lu - - - jah. Hal - le - lu -

row the boat a - shore, Hal - le - lu - - - jah. Hal - le - lu -

- - - jah._____

- - - jah._____

12. Oh! Susanna

Traditional
Arr. Philip Lawson

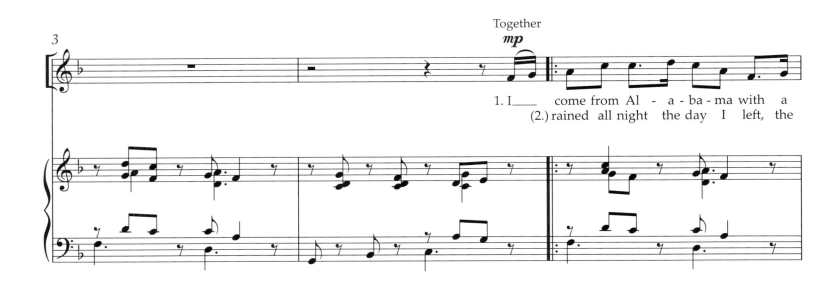

Together

1. I___ come from Al - a - ba - ma with a
(2.) rained all night the day I left, the

ban - jo on my knee; I'm__ goin' to Lou' - si - a - na, my true love for to see.
wea - ther it was dry; The__ sun so hot I froze to death; Su - san - na don't you cry.

13. Shenandoah

Traditional
Arr. Philip Lawson

1. Oh, Shen-an-doah,__ I long to see you;____ A-
(2.) Oh, Shen-an-doah,__ I love your daugh-ter;____ A-

1. Oh, Shen-an-doah,__ I long to see you;____ A-
(2.) Oh, Shen-an-doah,__ I love your daugh-ter;____ A-

-way____ you rol-ling riv-er.____ Oh Shen-an-doah,____ I long to
-way____ you rol-ling riv-er.____ For her I'd cross____ your roam-ing

-way____ you rol-ling riv-er.____ Oh Shen-an-doah,____ I long to
-way____ you rol-ling riv-er.____ For her I'd cross____ your roam-ing

14. Swanee River

Traditional
Arr. Philip Lawson

1. Way down u - pon the Swan - ee Ri - ver, Far, far a -
2. All up and down the whole cre - a - tion, Sad - ly I

-way, That's where my heart is turn-ing ev - er, That's where the old folks stay.
roam, Still long-ing for the old plan - ta-tion, And for the old folks at home.

Voice 1
Ev' - ry-where is sad and drear - y, ev' - ry-where I roam,

Voice 2
Ev' - ry-where is sad and drear - y, ev' - ry - where I roam,

15. She's Like the Swallow

Traditional
Arr. Philip Lawson

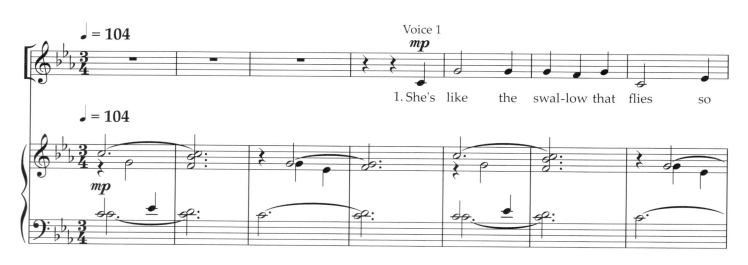

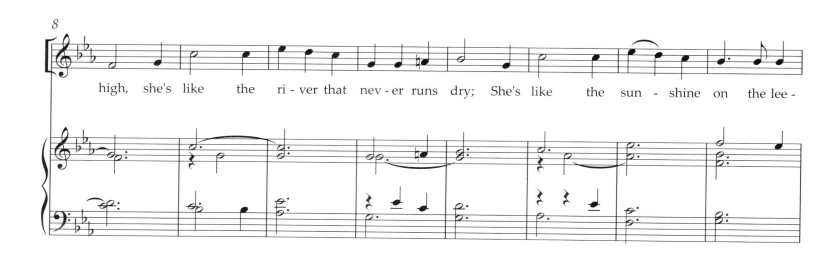

(Voice 1)

oo oo

Voice 2
mp

2.'Twas out in the mea-dow this fair maid did go, A - pick-ing the love - ly

oo

cresc.

prim - rose. The more she picked the more she pulled, Un - til she

cresc.

3. She

gath-ered her a - pron full.

mf

5. How fool-ish, fool-ish you must be, To think I love__ no-

-one but thee; The world's not made__ for one a-lone, I take de-

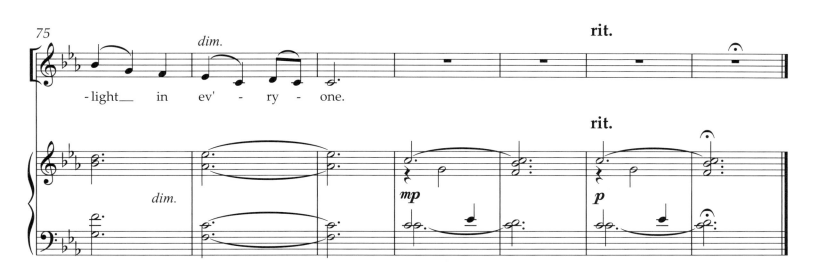

-light__ in ev'-ry-one.

16. Swing Low, Sweet Chariot

Traditional
Arr. Philip Lawson

17. The Gift to be Simple

Traditional
Arr. Philip Lawson

'Tis the gift to be sim-ple, 'tis the

gift to be free, 'tis the gift to come down where you ought to be. And when we find our-selves in a

place just right, 'twill be in the val-ley of love and de-light. When true sim-

18. The Riddle Song

Traditional
Arr. Philip Lawson

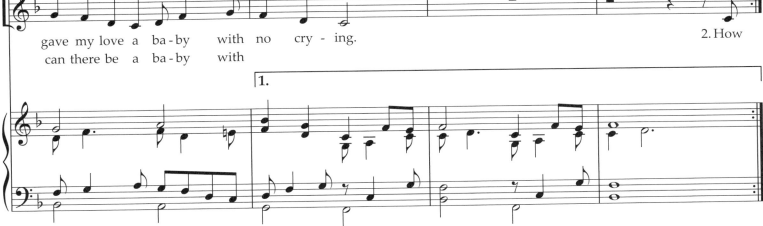

19. When Johnny Comes Marching Home

Traditional
Arr. Philip Lawson

men will cheer and the boys will shout, The la - dies they will all turn out,
vil - lage lads___ and las - sies say With ro - ses they will strew the way, } And we'll all feel gay when

12a
1. John-ny comes march-ing home.
2. The John-ny comes march-ing home.

13b Voice 1
3. Get rea - dy for the Ju - bi - lee, Hur - ra!___ hur - ra! We'll
(4.) love and friend-ship on that day, Hur - ra!___ hur - ra! Their

Voice 2
3. Get rea - dy for the Ju - bi - lee, Hur - ra!___ hur - ra! We'll
(4.) love and friend-ship on that day, Hur - ra!___ hur - ra! Their

20. Yankee Doodle

Traditional
Arr. Philip Lawson

Yan-kee Doo-dle came to town a - ri-ding on a po-ny; He stuck a fea-ther in his cap and called it mac-a-ro - ni.

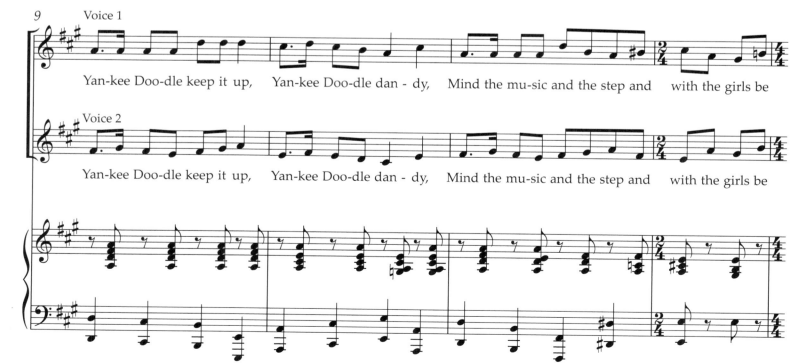

Voice 1
Yan-kee Doo-dle keep it up, Yan-kee Doo-dle dan - dy, Mind the mu-sic and the step and with the girls be

Voice 2
Yan-kee Doo-dle keep it up, Yan-kee Doo-dle dan - dy, Mind the mu-sic and the step and with the girls be